These are the

Rhymes

of my Life

Barbara,

Hope you enjoy

my Rhymes

Deb Ul

These are the Rhymes of my Life

Dale Wilson

TATE PUBLISHING
AND ENTERPRISES, LLC

Published by Tate Publishing & Enterprises, LLC
127 E. Trade Center Terrace | Mustang, Oklahoma 73064 USA
1.888.361.9473 | www.tatepublishing.com

Tate Publishing is committed to excellence in the publishing industry. The company reflects the philosophy established by the founders, based on Psalm 68:11,
"The Lord gave the word and great was the company of those who published it."

Book design copyright © 2016 by Tate Publishing, LLC. All rights reserved.
Cover design by Joshua Rafols
Interior design by Gram Telen

Published in the United States of America

ISBN: 978-1-68270-107-2
1. Poetry / Subjects & Themes / General
2. Poetry / American / General
16.01.20

Contents

Love

Tributes/Dedications

Life/Liberty

Nature

Inspirational

Self

To My Wife

Susan

(First poem written to my wife)

To a lady I deeply appreciate
And cherish as I've never done
A little poem I wish to dictate
To prove my love she has won

The more I am without you
Shows me how much I really care
'Cuz my thoughts are always about you
And I hope you're always there

I don't know why you love me
I really can't believe it is true
But whatever it is you see
I hope that you always do

Though my dreams of life are plenty
My ambitions for life are so few
Though my age is almost of twenty
I have no idea what I want to do

But if ever our love has an ending
If ever our ways have to part
You must know this one thing
I will always keep you close to my heart

(November 1979)

To You, Sue

To my sweetheart
To my hon'
You're so loving
You're so fun
A ray of sunlight
A drop of dew
All wonderful things
Go in harmony with you
I want you, babe
To share my dreams
And let our love flow
Like the mountain streams
For now, for always
From start, till end
Just be my love
Just be my friend
So here's a reminder
Just for you
Sending all my love
From me to you, Sue

(January 1981)

Keep Love Alive

So many times our hopes are stunted
Our dreams go unfulfilled
So many times our feelings are hidden
To leave nothing on which to build

It's hard to create the insight
To lead us down our path
To keep us close and true
To avoid both pain and wrath

There are too many doubts between us
About what lay ahead
To many unfounded quarrels
To many harsh words said

We must avoid the hatred
No matter what the cost
Even if we have to part
There must be no love lost

So tell me what you think
About what I have said
I'd rather leave while I love you
Than leave when our love is dead
(1982)

If It Wasn't for You

If it wasn't for you, Babe
I'd be much more
Than lonely and blue
For your love is so sweet
And your love is so true
I would be destitute
If it wasn't for you, Babe

But it's not just your love
Your caring for me
It's the way that you move me
The way you make me see

You really support me
And that's not a joke
If you didn't handle things
We'd be more than just broke

I know I don't deserve you
You are simply too good
I can't give the things
That a good husband would

Dale Wilson

Why you stick by me
I'll never ever know
But I'm more thankful
Than mere words can show

If it wasn't for you, Babe
I would be nowhere
I would be through
But with your love so sweet
And your love so true
My life has meaning
All because of you, Babe

(1985)

Together

Time flies by
We laugh, we cry
We've had to try
But we've done it all
TOGETHER

You're the one
Who makes it fun
We're on the run
And we've done it all
TOGETHER

Our wants, our dreams
Though different it seems
We're the best of teams
Letting us do it all
TOGETHER

If you ever leave
I will surely grieve
It'd be too hard to believe
We won't be doing it all
TOGETHER

So, my darling, Sue
No matter what you do
Be assured my Love is true
Let's always do it all
TOGETHER
(1990)

Sweetheart Day

Well here we are, my sweetheart
Sharing another sweetheart day
Though it hasn't been so easy
I think we've done okay

Oh yes, we've had our struggles
Ornery children and the like
The government taking all our money
Saying, "Get ready for another hike"

But we'll keep rolling with the punches
Together as a team
With any luck next sweetheart day
We'll be rolling in the green

I Love You, Babe
Of that be sure
An ounce of gold
Could not be as pure
(February 1998)

Tender Moments

The sun is shining
Through the windows of my mind
Leaving me happy
And with no sense of time

I love these moments
But they're only here
When I'm with you
And the reasons are clear

I love you as much
As these moments themselves
And I'll always have these moments
On my mind's shelves
(1988)

The Key

You are the Love of my Life
My one and only, my one so sweet
You are my reason for living
You make my whole world complete

I hope you are with me forever
My world will end if you ever go
To be in your arms inspires me
You allow my true love to flow

So always remember, my darling
That we must never part
To prove my love for you is true
I offer you the key to my heart
(April 2013)

Tied to Me

I'll take you to new highs
I'll get you through lows
I'll take you to those places
That nobody knows

You know you're the one
Who makes my life complete
No one could love me better
No love could be as sweet

I bequeath to you my very soul
Over my heart you've full control
No matter what the future brings
Our hearts are tied with invisible strings
(2011)

Anniversary Poem

(To My Wife, Susan)

As we travel together with the sands of time
Share these special moments, yours and mine
I know it's going to sound like a playboy line
But after all these years, you are still so fine

The way we've grown and trials we've had
Through troubled times when we've been mad
Through the hard times when we've been sad
We've made it through them, and I'm so glad

No one ever thought we would last this long
So many were sure that our love was wrong
But we have proven that together we belong
There is just no other love nearly as strong

As with this year, we will have so many more
Our love will be stronger than the year before
You will always remain the woman that I adore
I believe it's what God put me on this earth for

Happy anniversary, Sweetheart
Love ya bunches!
(October 2009)

A Poem for My Sweetheart on Her Birthday

Happy birthday to my sweet
To know you love me makes me complete
Every year together lets me see
You are most certainly the best part of me

I hope to celebrate many more
Each and every one better than the one before
You are my bright and shining light
You bring me comfort both day and night

I hope you have a special day
A special month and special year, I pray
Love you with all my heart, dear
Love you this, last, and every year

(2010)

To You

To find the answers that I seek
To remain contrite and meek
To be unequivocally true
To devote my life to you

You are the sum of my ambition
Never bring you cause for suspicion
To confirm your reason for belief
Never bring you pain or grief

I will live my life to please you
Make every effort to appease you
For every day I'm your companion
Is another day I'll always champion

From this moment until my final day
We'll endure any challenge sent our way
With my eyes to the heavens I will pray
That together forever we will stay

My darling, I promise you this
With each and every sweet kiss
You are my reason for living
To you my heart I'm giving
(2014)

To Thirty with Love

You've been my rock
The essence of my life
Everything a man could ask for
In a partner and a wife

It's been thirty years now
Can you believe it is true
We've beaten all the odds
We've shown what love can do

We've conquered our troubles
Overcome so many doubts
We've shown the entire world
What true love is all about

The life we've made together
Has been solid and secure
The way we handle hard times
Proves that our love is pure

We've always belonged together
We're lost when we're apart
We compliment each other's soul
We'll always be joined at the heart

I just can't wait to see what
The next thirty have in store
Because I'm sure that every year
I will love you even more
(October 2014)

Our Love

You are the best of me
Forget about the rest of me
I believe in destiny
For you to be here with me

You are my bright sunshine
My darlin', you are so fine
I think about you all the time
I am in awe that you are mine

You are my queen and I your king
Bless the day you took my ring
With you I can do anything
Our love makes my heart sing

The Sun, the Moon, the Stars
And the whole wide world is ours
As we travel both near and far
By plane, train, boat or car

Stay with me forever
We must always be together
Our two hearts are tethered
And any storm, our love can weather
(2014)

Only You for Me

To see the light in your eye
The wonder of your sight
To never have to question why
To just know that it is right

It was always only you for me
Never a single doubt in my mind
It is just how it was meant to be
To not see it, you'd have to be blind

We'll share the road of life together
Navigate it forever hand in hand
Together, forever, come whatever
No need for anyone to understand

A toast to you, my sweet soul mate
Here is to sharing this life as one
I look forward to whatever our fate
A life worth living when it is done
(August 2015)

If You Could See

If only you could see you
See your beauty with my eyes
You'd see what the truth is
That I am telling you no lies

It is not just your beauty without
It's the amazing beauty within
To tell you how much I love you
There are so many places to begin

You make the whole world brighter
With you it's a better place to live
You shine beauty on so many people
To each a bit of your soul you give

The way you make me better
Care for me and you love me so
You'll never see the magnitude
The effect you have, you'll never know

Unless you could really see you
With eyes from the other side
The beauty that you project outward
Can't be explained although I've tried

So even though I tell you every day
Try to make you believe every night
I guess you'll have to take it on faith
Looking at you, the beauty in my sight
(2015)

With You

When I look into your eyes
I see what dreams are made of
This is so much more than lust
I know this could only be love

When you walk into a room
I can feel your beauty surround
I can feel you before I see you
And my heart begins to pound

I've just got to have you with me
I'm so happy that you are mine
You make my life worth living
My heaven on earth so divine

Say you'll stay with me forever
Say our love will always be true
I have got to make you believe
My world begins and ends with you

(July 2015)

Forgive Me

The trouble that I've caused you
The pain I've put you through
For you to still stand beside me
Tells me your love is true

I want so much to do better for you
To be the man you deserve
I promise I'm trying every day
To assure this love I preserve

Believe that I truly love you
Rest assured I really do care
I want that our time together
Is the rest of our lives to share

Please forgive me my mistakes
And trust I'm learning every day
To be a good husband to you forever
In each and every way

Love you, sweetheart

(2013)

My Portrait of You

Can a poem paint a picture?
Can a picture tell a rhyme?
The words floating in my head
Paint a picture in my mind

It's a picture of such beauty
Of sweetness and God's grace
And the subject of the picture
A crystal clear image of your face

I am so blessed and fortunate
That he brought you into my life
There is not a man in this world
That could have found a better wife

You bring warmth and sunshine
On those cold and dark dreary days
You take me to the top of a mountain
Where I can bask in the heat of the rays

I know I don't always make it clear
Tell you how much you mean to me
But if my words could paint a picture
I think it would then be so clear to see

For all the years we have been together
For all the love that has been conveyed
I want to show you my appreciation
In this portrait of words I have made

Happy 31st, my love
(2015)

Love

My Dreams for You

If I could have my dreams come true
Every dream would be of you
I'd want to sleep both night and day
I would dream my whole life away

Only you can make my dreams be real
Please tell me that the same you feel
We'll be together, no need to sleep
I'm giving you my dreams to keep

My heart is yours to have, to hold
To sculpture, shape, and to mold
Just please know that it's not a toy
It's yours forever to enjoy
(2013)*

---

* This poem was written for or inspired by inmates at a facility
where I work as a correctional officer.

Starting Over

I know we've had our hard times, girl
Our fights and arguments too
But to have made through all of that
You know our love must be true

We just need to make a fresh start
We need to let go of our past
If we could only forgive each other
We could build a life that can last

So believe me when I say I love you
Believe I want us to start anew
Believe that you're the woman for me
Believe that I'm the man for you
(2014)*

---

*   This poem was written for or inspired by inmates at a facility
where I work as a correctional officer.

The Colors of Our Love

We've always got each other seeing red
We spend all of our time feeling blue
We're consumed and green with jealousy
This war can ruin our love so true

We both have our own checkered pasts
Many regrets we'd like to black out
We've got to let go of what was
Or forever have our love be in doubt

Let's get out from under the gray skies
Get out into the bright yellow sun
Learn to believe in each other
Believe my heart you have won

Let's stop beating each other black-and-blue
Stop making each other bleed bright red
Let's bury our past deep in the brown dirt
Or we could be burying our love instead

From this day forward let's start fresh
Let the rain wash away what is past
Let the colors of the rainbow shine on us
And promise each other our love will last
(2014)*

---

* This poem was written for or inspired by inmates at a facility
where I work as a correctional officer.

Wait for Me

I can't believe this is my life
Now it's done, I'm in the pen
The fun is over, I've messed it up
And I can't do it over again

There was a time it was so easy
I was so big and bulletproof
Now the Meth has done me in
And I have concrete for a roof

I can't even begin to tell you, love
How sorry I am for all the pain
To hurt you and what we have
It just almost drives me insane

To miss all the years of growing up
Of our sweet, precious little baby
I just hope and pray that you can wait
And somehow find a way to forgive me

Every day I'll think of you both
Dream about you every night
Count down the days till I come home
So our sweet family can reunite

Please wait for me, my Darling
You are my world, my life
Until I can come back to you and her
And I can take you as my wife
(2013)*

---

* This poem was written for or inspired by inmates at a facility
where I work as a correctional officer.

My Light

There is a light in my life
She shines brightly on me
Of all the hardships I face
It is her who lets me see

Please don't ever doubt my love
Please know that it is true
I can make it through anything
If I can make it through to you

This is for you, sweet darling
This is my pledge from my heart
When I am free to be with you
A new life will be ours to start

I think of you every day
I dream of you every night
It feels so good to me
To have you as my light
(2013)*

---

* This poem was written for or inspired by inmates at a facility
where I work as a correctional officer.

Ocean of Love

As a sailor would love the sea
To you I express my love
As we navigate the ocean of life
Being guided by the stars up above

You are a being to be cherished
You are a sacred vessel of life
You are the mother of my child
I pray you are soon to be my wife

I must recover from my indiscretions
Bring my ship around and sail true
Set myself a course for calmer waters
Then I will sail right home to you

Let me bring you to the cabin
There we will chart our course to sail
We will sail these seas forever
There is no way our love can fail
(2014)*

---

* This poem was written for or inspired by inmates at a facility
where I work as a correctional officer.

Only You

I know my past belies me
I know I've been untrue
I've got to make you see
I'm now living just for you

What can I do to prove it
Make you believe again
Any mountain, I will move it
Any challenge I will win

I'll do whatever it takes
To restore your trust in me
I'm done with past mistakes
This is who I want to be

So please believe in us
A future, a family, a home
Please let go of all that was
And I'll never leave you alone
(2014)*

---

* This poem was written for or inspired by inmates at a facility
where I work as a correctional officer.

It's Over

It's like the setting sun
That time when the day is done
When you wish it could go on
But all the light is gone

You want to make it better
Some way to make it last forever
But it's just as a dying rose
When an early fall it has froze

Our love has just run its course
There's no sense to make it worse
There was a time my heart you won
But I'm sorry to say that time is done

We have to go our separate ways
There'd only be more heartache if I stay
So with this I tell you good-bye
I pray short be the time you cry
(2013)*

---

*   This poem was written for or inspired by inmates at a facility
where I work as a correctional officer.

Love Is a Thing

Love is a thing
That can't be borrowed
It can't be given away
Love is a thing
You have to feel
When the right one comes your way

Love is a thing
That can't be misused
It can't be thrown around
Love is a thing
Just lying in hiding
Waiting to be found

Love is a thing
That I am feeling
For a person whom I know
Love is a thing
I hope she returns
And lets the feelings flow
(1976)

Look Forward

You tell me of your troubles past
And troubles on their way
But your peace will come at last
On one bright and glorious day

I wish that I could comfort you
If only I knew how
I wish so hard you won't be blue
As you are right now

You must think of a future bright
And your past must be forgot
You must think that all is right
And you must care a lot

I leave you now, oh faithful friend
To start my life anew
And up the road around the bend
Is a better life for you
(1975)

Especially for Nancy

My——life is too short
Love——cannot be
Forever——a handicap
To——a man like me
My——life is mine to guide
Nancy——you will see
Take——your time in life
Care——will make you free

You are a girl
I won't forget
The greatest girl
I've ever met

I've known you now
For quite some time
Long enough to love you
And wish you were mine

But I can't have you
And that is okay
Because for your forever friendship
Is all I pray
(1976)

Annie May

Down by the old creek
Dreamin' an hour away
Dream about a rosy cheek
The one of Annie May

Annie May, you are sunshine
As sweet as morning dew
How I wish you were still mine
Annie May, I love you

We were so very close
Like birds of a feather
Until the wind of hate rose
And our love hit bad weather

So she left me all alone
And went with another man
I guess I will just go home
And forget her if I can

Down by the old creek
Dreamin' an hour away
Dreams that make me feel weak
My dreams of Annie May
(1975)

For Love

For the love of life
For the love of living
For the time with loved ones
For the love they're giving

It's this love we live for
Cherish each and every day
That makes us who we are
What we do and what we say

May I always feel this love
Way down deep in my heart
Be it while we are together
Or those times we spend apart

For a love that lasts forever
For a love that fills a lifetime
For a love that brightens every day
For a love like yours and mine
(2014)

Baby

(Just for Fun)

Baby, let me tell	you
My love for you is	true
Baby, don't make me	blue
By telling me we are	through
Don't you ever be a	hater
Oh, baby, you are so	gangster
I am not being a	player
And I'll never be a	betrayer
To be alone with you I	pray
Think about you night and	day
There is nothing more I can	say
Come on, baby, let's	play
You and me always be	tight
You know that it just feels	right
Want to show you my moves	tonight
We'll be grooving till morning	light
	(2014)

Love Both Ways

Can——a man be 10 feet tall?

I——know I feel that tall

Love——has come over me and

You——are the one I call.

More?—and more I think of you

I——will now tell you all,

Think—of how I wrote this poem

Not——the words across at all.
(1976)

Stay

You say you're leaving, going away
Tell me what I can do, what I can say
Whatever it takes, Babe, to make you stay

Stay, to make my world complete
Stay, no other love could be as sweet
Stay, so I can devote my life to you
Stay, so I can prove my love is true

I've done you wrong, I've been untrue
But that was, oh, so long before I knew
Just how deep I was in love with you

Stay, to make my world complete
Stay, no other love could be as sweet
Stay, so I can devote my life to you
Stay, so I can prove my love is true

We can't throw away all these years
We can't have wasted all these tears
May the Lord above, my prayer he hears

Stay, to make my world complete
Stay, no other love could be as sweet
Stay, so I can devote my life to you
Stay, so I can prove my love is true

It's always been you right from the start
Life is not worth living if we're apart
So please don't leave and break my heart

Stay, to make my world complete
Stay, no other love could be as sweet
Stay, so I can devote my life to you
Stay, so I can prove my love is true
Stay

(July 2015)

Tonight

We got the jukebox rippin' it
On the dance floor whippin' it
On fire tonight, we're doin' it right

You and me we're groovin' it
Makin' moves and smoothin' it
We're lyin' low, lettin' it flow

When trouble comes, I'm kickin' it
My armor don't have a nick in it
You mess with me, you will see

. . . .

Keeping time with the lights
Everything just feels so right
I'm giving you the best of me
I think this must be destiny

Later tonight we'll lie as one
Let me show you how it's done
I want to feel your smooth caress
This night will end in sweet success

We could make this night last forever
Spend the rest of our lives together
You and I could live life as one
Wake up each day with the rising sun

This could be it, who knows
Let's just see where it goes
If I could make you mine
That would be oh so fine
(August 2015)

Tributes/Dedications

Father

(For My Dad)

A Father, a Husband
A Provider and Friend
Stricken with an Illness
Our Love Couldn't mend

We send our Love with him
To a sweet and peaceful place
And keep our memories of him
To hold and forever embrace

A man of Silence
A man so Proud
A man so Quiet
Can be missed so Loud
(1990)

To Mom

(For My Mom)

There were no clues it was your time
No hint of what was to come
We were blind to the seriousness
The damage your illness had done

On a cold December day
We lost a piece of our heart
You left us without warning
No idea you were to depart

A Mother, a Sister, a Friend
A glimmer, a spark of hope
May the Lord help us heal
Give us the strength to cope

We didn't get that final moment
To share those feelings so true
Through our prayers we say "Good-bye"
Through him we say "I Love You"

Think of you and miss you forever!
Your loving son and your entire family
(December 1, 2006)

Taylor

(To Aaron and Kerri)

To your sweet new jewel
Proof of life's renewal
To a love so profound
Proof your love is sound

Here's from us to you
Wishes sincere and true
For this sweet new life
Be free of pain and strife

If you've ever a need
Call on us indeed
For our family's newest player
We'll do anything—for Taylor
(October 2000)

Unexpected Blessing
Taylor's Little Kenyon

(My Great-Grandson)

You arrived so fast, what a surprise
But here you are, a special little guy
To see the pride in your Mother's eyes
It is no longer for us to question why

You were sent to us by the Lord above
He alone knows the reasons you are here
It is only for us to show you great love
Keep you from harm, take away your fear

We look forward to watching you grow
Seeing again how life happens so fast
Becoming a young man before we know
Wishing we could make your childhood last

Be sure to take your time, my little man
Make the most out of each and every day
Be happy and have as much fun as you can
Laugh and sing, run and ride, and play

Above all, always know we are here for you
Here to make your life as sweet as it can be
To show you a family love so deep and true
Provide the best of the world for you to see

—Papa
(November 2014)

Sierra

The first granddaughter from our youngest son
You have grown to be so loving and so fun
It's been such a pleasure just watching you grow
Becoming more mature, your beauty, your glow

The years go by so quickly, you've grown so fast
I wish there was a way, to make your childhood last
My true wish for you in all the years to come
Is you achieve a happiness never realized by some

Always work toward your goals and ambitions
Listen to your heart and follow your intuitions
I'm hoping all your dreams for your life come true
Remember, Grandma and Papa will always love you

Papa
(2015)

Kenzie

Here's a little rhyme for McKenzie Marie
Our sweet Granddaughter number three
She's just as sweet as sweet can be
With lots of love for her Grandma and me

We miss getting to see you nearly every day
Watching you grow, the games you play
When you come to visit, we want you to stay
The good-byes are hard when you go away

So we want you to know that we cherish you
Always remember in everything you do
That we are praying all your dreams come true
With all our love, Papa Dale and Grandma Sue

(2015)

Newfound Love

(To My Father-in-Law and His New Bride)

When they met, they were each
At crossroads in their life
She had lost her husband
And he had lost his wife

The loyalty and commitment they showed
For loved ones who had gone
Just increased their respect and trust
That their love would be strong

In each other they found a way
To deal with their daily sorrows
And within each other's eyes and arms
Look forward to brighter tomorrows

He was her knight in shining armor
She, his lovely blossoming flower
To her he was the brave hero
Come to rescue her from her tower

Their love has grown so quickly
You know it has to be right
It's brought back their vibrance
It's rekindled their inner light

You can tell when you look at Willard
In his eye that familiar "twinkle"
When he popped the question and
Lois agreed to become "Mrs. Hinkle"

So we send them to continue
On this journey of their lives
Which I foresee to be sweet and peaceful
Well...except when Lois drives!!

She runs pedal to the metal
He sets a slightly slower pace
But no matter what their speed
Together they'll win this race
(April 2001)

Wade

He was such a quiet, caring person
A father, son, brother, cousin, and friend
To all of his relationships and ties
He was honest and true to the end

The frightful things his body endured
Our faith and patience do thou test
To know his heart and soul go to you
Once his earthly body is laid to rest

The harrowing, mysterious, evil things
That shakes us to our very core
We must rejoice and trust in you
That the pain and suffering will be no more

It seems so soon you've called him home
A very difficult decision you have made
To leave us here to miss him so
To continue life without our Wade

Please make a comfortable place for him
And rejoin him with those who passed before
I believe he's earned a special place with you
When you welcome him through heaven's door

I'll remember and keep you close forever
Your cousin, Dale
(June 2009)

Michelle

A loving daughter, mother, and sister
Companion, cousin, and friend
To know her journey in life is over
Is just so hard for us to comprehend

So young and so full of energy
Inspirational just with her touch
Our lives better to have known her
She has enriched them oh so much

She was the essence of positive
Her spirit bright and forever shining
Within any storm or dark cloud
She became that silver lining

We will miss her oh so dearly
Our lives will never be the same
But those many precious memories
In our thoughts will always remain

The good Lord has called her home
To watch over us all from above
For the rest of our own lives
I'm sure we'll always feel her love
(September 2014)

For Sheila

She was always the shy one
So timid and sincere
Whenever she would speak
Only the truth you'd hear

She never knew her true worth
How much she really meant
The friendship she provided
And all the Love she spent

The good times we had together
We'll always hold so dear
We had no idea back then
Of the trouble drawing near

The illness that she battled
Seemed so cruel and wrong
The time it took from her
Still proved she was so strong

The fight is finally over
At last free from the pain
We'll always love and miss you
Our true friend Sheila Jane
(September 2010)

Kevin

I want to tell you
About a real good friend
Who has helped me out
Again and again

This dude's cool
His name is Kevin
He makes my life
Seem like heaven

Kevin, this poem
Is all for you
To bring you luck
In whatever you do
(1980)

Garfield

I've never been much of a "cat person" per say
But Garfield was an "old soul" from the start
It didn't take very long at all sixteen years ago
Before he had taken full control of my heart

We had much in common for a man and a cat
He was practical, reserved, and lazy just like me
He wasted no energy on silly, frivolous things
And he lived up to the name of Garfield to a tee

Today we had to say good-bye to our dear friend
A piece of our soul, a dear companion gone away
We take the comfort he's now in a better place
And our precious memories will be here to stay

Gone now is his discomfort, pain, and suffering
He can walk easy again, and his spirit is set free
He'll kick back on the arm of the good Lord's chair
And keep watch over his sweet Susan and me

Love ya, little buddy!

(August 2015)

Missy

Today we say good-bye to a loyal pet
We are relieved and yet so upset
It was the worst trip ever to the vet
In memory of our loving Missy

Even though we knew her time was near
It's so hard to hold back the flow of tears
She's been a companion so many years
We'll always remember our Missy

She picked us as her owners long ago
A more faithful pet we will never know
She just came to us and would never go
Our loving little girl Missy

She was so protective and yet so sweet
Never wandered farther than down the street
No chains or pens we would ever need
That was our dog Missy

A great admission through Heaven's gate
The Lord has gained a wonderful mate
By his side I know that she will wait
Until that day we join our Missy
(2013)

Hope

You helped give me such a nice life
You always treated me so good
And when I started feeling sickly
You did everything you could

Taking me out for my walkies
Spending time out in the yard
Through my time of suffering
I know it had to be so hard

When storms were loud and scary
And outside it was pouring rain
You kept me in comfort downstairs
Always helping to ease my pain

The way you cared for me
The way you showed me love
Know I'm smiling down on you
With the good Lord up above

Although my name is Hope,
Hope is what you gave me
This is to my Jim and Lois
For helping set my spirit free

(September 2011)

Dale Wilson

My Circle of Friends

One of the tests of true friendship is time
And time has proven there are no friends truer than mine
Though we are so different, we are the same
We always share each other's sorrows and pain
Though we are separate, we are still one
We share all the good times and all the fun
Though we are apart we remain together
We endure distance as would birds of a feather
I feel so very blessed in this part of my life
As blessed as I was when I received the love of my wife
And I want you all to know
No matter which direction our lives go
That if you really need me, I'll be there
I would make my way to you anywhere
I hold all of you dear to my heart
And nothing can ever tear that apart
(September 2012)

The Gang

This poem is for the gang
To some we're just a pain
But we enjoy our fun
It's better with more than one

We like each other rather well
And most people can really tell
We're together most of the time
Playing games with quarters and dimes

We've won our battles, most of them
We'd probably do them all again
For life's for fun and fun's for us
I don't know why people have to fuss

Well, I guess I better end this now
And show to the rest, oh wow
You know life's been good to me
Most of the time as you can see

A toast to the gang
Who, to me, is not a pain
(1976)

Mr. Sidwell

As you leave to start anew
Just wanted you to know
Our best wishes are here for you
To take with you when you go

May success come right away
May your profit numbers soar
We all just want to say to you
Never forget what came before

So long to you, Mr. Sidwell
Keep us near to your heart
We bid you a fond farewell
As this new adventure you start
(2007)

Farewell to Herb's

"The best hamburgers in town"
It's not just a catchy phrase
It's real truth in advertising
A legacy deserving of praise

Dating back five decades
It's been the best place to eat
As long as I've been around
Herb's is where we'd meet

But more than just a burger joint
More than just a place to go
Gary has cared about the people
His sincerity would always show

He's been there for my family
A dedicated and caring friend
This is such a loss to the community
A tradition has come to an end

This is to you, Mr. Whitehurst
It's so hard to find the words
To tell you how much we'll miss you
Garden City won't be the same without HERB'S
(2014)

Mom

You brought me into the world
You did everything that you could
I owe my whole being to you
But I still haven't lived like I should

I want to be a man you are proud of
A man to the world and a better son
I want to make up for my mistakes
To repay you for all that you've done

You have my love now and forever
My dedication for as long as I live
To be there whenever you need me
Anything I have, to you I would give

The good Lord will save me through you
You will both help change my behavior
You're more than a mom, you're a friend
You're more than a friend, you're my savior
(2013)*

---

* This poem was written for or inspired by inmates at a facility where I work as a correctional officer.

My True Friend

To my friend and confidant
Always there for me to share
You are more than I could want
Just because I know you care

There is nothing like a friend so true
What I need in my life right now
Words can't express what I owe you
I pray that time will let me show you

A love based on our friendship
Based on our mutual trust
A true and caring relationship
So sincere, without greed or lust

Thank you so much for your heart
Thanks for your promise and letters
For this journey I'm about to start
No other could support me better
(2014)*

---

* This poem was written for or inspired by inmates at a facility
where I work as a correctional officer.

Tribute to Dale Earnhardt

My tribute to the memory of Dale
My salute to the Man in Black
I admired him through good and bad
I thought him to be the best on the track

Though he is no longer with us
His influence still has an effect
On the way that I view the sport
And how I felt our spirits connect

On the last lap of the big race
Expectations of that number eight
Though you were taken before you got it
The only thing that stopped you was fate

He had the desire and determination
I could only wish I had the half of
He risked losing his all, his everything
To excel at what he truly loved

To run flat out and on the edge
Yet maintain that degree of control
The wide open roar of his engine
Connecting directly with his soul

The intimidator in the black #3
The stamina no one could match
The steel nerves and laser eyes
The legend no one will ever catch
(August 2001)

Life/Liberty

A Single Soldier

Jim and I were checkin' the lines
Tom and Cory were on the side
We knew that soon we'd have to fight
It was a fact we couldn't hide

The lines were secure and holdin' tight
But the fear was showing in all
I knew that soon our nerves would break
If we didn't hear that battle call

Our wondering minds were answered soon
By a shot from who knows where
And after that, all hell broke out
We were firing without a care

Then suddenly I felt a sting
That knocked me out of place
Oh! The fear and pain I felt
As blood trickled down my face

I called for help but no one heard
For what seemed like years
I called until I couldn't speak
And my eyes were filled with tears

When they finally came to help
I knew that I would die
And the only thing that puzzled me
Is no one there knew why

It won't be long till life is gone
And I'll leave this dreary earth
That has bound me like a chain
Since the day of my birth

Why do people have to die
In these fatal and hateful wars
There are excuses but not reasons
To what these deaths are for

All the men who start these wars
Should have to fight alone
Then maybe there'd be less of them
And the men could all come home

The pain is sharp, my sight is blurred
And I can barely see to write
I am surprised I've lived this long
And hope is still in sight

But I just now heard the doctor say
I think we've lost this man
But he's really trying to live
And fighting all he can

He said he's surprised to see
That I am still quite alive
"But even though he's lived this long
I don't think he'll survive"

All men say they hate to fight
But still the wars go on
I'm writing now without sight
So I'll have to say, "So long"
(1976)

As If I Were There

Here I am so far from home
Fighting in this desert storm
I feel so lost and all alone
Answering the call of freedom

The only thing that keeps me sane
Is knowing the fight is not in vain
My people at home are sharing the pain
Answering the call of freedom

When all is over, said and done
And we know that freedom is won
When the smoke has cleared from the sun
And we've answered the call of freedom

I can go home with head held high
Look at my people eye to eye
There'll be no need for me to cry
'Cuz I answered the call of freedom

I am an American, true and proud
I'll tell the world right out loud
To the most disbelieving crowd
That America is the call of freedom
(1991)

Feelings

Tears
Flowing steady
Years
Gone already

Love
Give it a try
Dove
Flying high

Dreams
Good and bad
Teams
Games you've had

Life
Not that long
Strife
Weak and strong

Hate
Always present
Mate
Always pleasant

Smiles
Now and then
Miles
Start over again

Tears
Flowing steady
Years
Gone already
(1976)

Good Thing Gone

Where are we going?
What destiny awaits?
Are we just lost souls?
Is it already too late?

We live in an age now
Of mediocrity and mundane
We champion just average
To excel is deemed insane

We no longer have discipline
No moral compass to guide
Too much of the population
Just along for the free ride

Our schools no longer teach
To be the best of the best
They're only getting taught
To be as good as the rest

Once the best in the world
In every category known
Every child made to strive
To be a success on their own

Now it's as long as you show up
Do the very minimum required
With our goals as lax as this
How can anyone be inspired?

Have we lost our determination?
Has our spirit been broken?
Where we once had that drive
Are we now just a token?

It seems to simply suggest
That we try to raise the bar
Is asking way too much
It's taking things too far

We must again strive to win
Have only one ~~first place~~ first-place prize
We can't just simply participate
And expect this country to rise

Bring back the glory
Change our current fate
We must better ourselves
Or it will be too late
(2015)

Live and Learn

Live and learn
Lose and gain
Give and receive
Joy and pain

Have a feeling
Have a thought
Sometimes right
Sometimes not

Always willing
Always game
In the end
It's still the same

Good luck, bad luck
Take a chance
It could ruin
It could enhance

Live and learn
Lose and gain
Give and receive
But not in vain
(1976)

Lovelight

Today is the best time
To love your friend and foe
And this poem was written
To let my lovelight show

Take your neighbors by the hand
And lead them to that light
Of kindness down deep inside
That you always hide from sight

Come on, people, boys and girls
Gather together hand in hand
And let your brilliant lovelight
Shine brightly across the land

Light all the towns and cities
All the countrysides and valleys
Brighten up all the ghettos
Lighten dark and lonely alleys

Get together now, one and all
With a blessing from Heaven above
There has never been any light
Brighter than the light of love

So come on, people, boys and girls
Gather together hand in hand
And let your brilliant lovelight
Shine brightly across the land
(1975)

My Father, Not My Dad

Since I was a younger man
We've never seen eye to eye
And it has become my true belief
That you will never even try

We've never had that connection
If we did, it has come undone
Never had the love that should be
Between a father and his son

I know I've made my share of mistakes
My judgment is not always the best
But you should be there to support me
Not just have me placed under arrest

I can only hope sometime in your life
Maybe you will come to see the light
That the relationship you had with me
Was just never loving and never right
(2014)*

---

* This poem was written for or inspired by inmates at a facility
where I work as a correctional officer.

No Friend of the Forward

In this fast-paced world
We all live day to day
We all have our struggles
With little time to play

We use our computers
To keep us in touch
With friends and family
Whom we love so much

So if you want to claim
To be a friend of mine
I was just wondering
If you would be so kind

As to never send me a forward
That has to be read
Then sent on to others
So I won't be found dead

Or to have years of bad luck
Or be forever in exile
Because I didn't forward
To 10 or more e-mails in my file

A true friend of mine
Wouldn't wish me such pain
They wouldn't get me involved
In some silly chain

So please take this to heart
I don't mean to offend
You can send it on if you like
Or you can just let it end

No matter what you do
I wish you the best
No bad luck should befall you
And this is sure not a test

Now if it's a joke
Or funny picture or such
I really enjoy those
So I won't make a fuss

So send me any news
That's from you to me
But if it's just some chain letter
That's a forward I'd rather not see
(2008)

Our Time

No time left to us
For the beauty of life
The world is past its prime
Full of struggle and strife

We have wasted so much
Of what should be so dear
With no consideration
For any later year

We're headed for damnation
Our time is running out
Unless we change our habits
And turn our course about
(March 1976)

Politics

In a world of harsh realities
Of clashing personalities
Dreams both sweet and cynical
Can we ever reach the pinnacle?

We are governed by men of greed
For profit our interests they concede
Making policies without common sense
Taking for themselves, passing on the expense

It's time to break the cycle
To end all that's senseless and maniacal
Take out the fuss and complication
And create a simpler situation

A world besieged
A world on fire
A world to be destroyed
By our own desire
(1977)

Saddam, Saddam

(Poem was written during the Gulf War for a friend who was serving during that time)

Saddam, Saddam
This ain't Vietnam
My man Hussein
You are insane
And you're going to go down

A fact you have to face
You are a total disgrace
You're Hitler in disguise
That's just not too wise
And you're going to go down

It's not just the USA
That's going to make you pay
You'll be punished by the Lord
On that you can take my word
And you're going to go down

Before it gets too late
You'd better change your fate
Before too many die
Just ask yourself why
You forced yourself to go down

—Just pack it up and get out of town—
—Because you're going to go down—
(1991)

School Subjects

Math
The tale of Math
Is easy to tell
If you know numbers
You'll do very well

English
We learn our English
In so many ways
And how it's changed
All through the days

History
The mystery of History
Is already solved
It tells of the way
We have evolved

Gym
Gym is a fun place
But sometimes it's not
Like when you're running
And working a lot

Art
In Art you draw
And make things with clay
And if they are good
You will get an "A"

Drafting
What you do in drafting
Is hard to explain
You draw an entire house
And sign on your name

Study Hall
In Study Hall you do
Your homework and such
And if you have lots
It helps very much
(1975)

Signs of Terror

Signs of terror
Old and New
Feeling Anguished
Feeling Blue

Live and learn
Through pain and strife
Call it heartbreak
Call it——Life

Look for the upbeat
Yearn for the best
Outdo the good ones
Outdo the best

Signs of terror
Old and New
It's up to you
To know what to do
(1988)

The Drunk

Not really knowing what to do
No place to go, no one to turn to
Have another drink, no one will know
But isn't this the way the story goes?

Just a drunk lying on a sidewalk
No one but himself with whom to talk
No reason to be sober, no roles to play
Just sit in contemplation, think of a better day

Once a ripe young man, full of life and love
But then time flew by, like a fleeing dove
Now a drunk old man lying on a sidewalk
No one but himself with whom to talk
(1976)

The Fate of *World Glory*

This story starts on a beautiful day
When a gigantic tanker was leaving the bay
Old *World Glory* was the tanker's name
And this is how its destruction came

She left the bay right on time
She was sailing smooth right down the line
They soon found out a storm was nigh
But they never thought any men would die

They hit the storm and the storm hit them
The waves kept coming again and again
Then the big one came, seventy feet tall
And picked up the ship, men and all

She cracked in the middle behind the bridge
And the oil she carried spilled over the ridge
As another wave hit, she broke in two
The few men left knew not what to do

The oil caught fire and tall grew the flame
Some men looked for shelter, then the others the same
When another wave hit, it put out the fire
The front end sank and the back wasn't much higher

The men they jumped, the few left alive
But to stay that way they would have to strive
Twenty-four hours later ten men were rescued
The rest of the forty the ocean subdued

So the legends were true, about the big waves
And the course they had sailed were many men's graves
Well, that's the end of this tragic story
Of the horrible fate of the tanker *World Glory*
(1975)

I Fear for America

Because more people are worried about controlling
guns than they are about controlling insane people!
Because Obama got reelected by people who say things
like, "I can't wait for Obamacare to take effect *because
it's free, right!*" and "Obama is one of the greatest
presidents ever because *he has spent the least money
of any president in history, right?*" (Actual quotes!)
Because it now takes almost as much money
to pay government wages as it does to pay
private sector wages! *Hello!* The private sector
has to pay the government's wages!
Because while we have people with no jobs, no homes,
no money, and no hope here at home, we're still sending
billions of dollars *we don't have* to foreign countries!
Because too many of these people with no jobs,
no homes, no money, and no hope don't want
a job, but expect the government or someone
else to give them a home, money, and hope.
Because it seems our morals and our need for
"political correctness" and trying to please every
weirdo in the country now greatly outweighs
our basic sense of *right* and *wrong!*

Because our people in government think they are above living by the same laws and programs they expect the very people they are supposed to be serving do!
Because while we used to be the best at nearly everything, we are now not the best at nearly anything!
God help America!
(2012)

Comical/Fun

Blue

Blue is what you see
On a sunny day
Blue is what you feel
When your lover goes away

Blue is what I like
More than all the rest
In case you ever ask me
Blue is the best

If you do not like it
I guess that's up to you
But just so you'll know
My favorite color is blue
(1974)

Dancing Days

I miss the days of my youth
Things just seemed more real
People connected one on one
It had a more personal feel

Guys would dance with girls
The music seemed so right
Now the girls just dance with girls
And the guys just want to fight

The lyrics had more meaning
They'd speak directly to your soul
I'd love to dance and sing along
To some classic rock and roll

I'd like to pour a little Coke
Into a big tall glass of rum
Add in a few shots of tequila
Get a little crazy, have a little fun

I don't understand the world today
The social network is a social bubble
Everyone's in their own little world
To be real is too much trouble

Bring back those glorious days
When people could really connect
Bring us back to a more simple life
So much more intimate and direct
(2015)

Daze of Drugs

Smokin' dope and shootin' up
Blowin' minds, eyes red, no sense
Music loud, but I can't hear it
All I know is I'm getting off by a fence

Wow, man, strange feelings
Flowin' through my brain
No matter how low I sit and stare
Nothin' stays the same

Dynamite! Just blew my mind
OD'in', freakin' out
Someone comin' after me
Don't know what it's all about

Cold turkey in an institute
Is what I'd call a bad trip
You're not awake half the time
And the other half you'll flip

Now I'm out and all right
I always thought I was real cool
But now I know how wrong I was
I was only a freakin' fool
(November 1976)

How to Catch a Woman

If you want to catch a woman
You first need to know what they are
They may be tall, short, skinny, or fat
They may be near or may be far

If you want to catch a woman
You have got to have a style
A certain way to catch their eye
And please them for a while

If you want to catch a woman
I wish you lots of luck
'Cuz even though they're hard to catch
Once you've caught them, you're stuck
(1975)

Limericks
(1975–76)

The Pie Guy

I once knew a fellow named Guy
Who would sit all day and eat pie
He'd eat three a day
To everyone he'd say
"I'll eat three a day till I die"

Out of Sorrow

I once knew a man deep in sorrow
Who thought there was no tomorrow
But he met someone nice
To his great surprise
Now he's no longer in sorrow

Old Man from Peru

There was an old man from Peru
Who dreamed he was caged in a zoo
He awoke feeling blue
It was then that he knew
That we're all caged up in a zoo

Harley

This is about a dog named Harley
He got lost in a big field of Barley
He wandered for hours
Through the barley towers
Until he found his master, Charlie

Trip to Hong Kong

There was a young boy named Tom
Who decided to go to Hong Kong
But he had to come back
The language he couldn't hack
So his stay was only two days long

Rich Bill

This story is about a man named Bill
He slipped while climbing a hill
He died coming down
Which excited the town
'Cuz they we all heirs to his will

Dishonest Sue

There was a young girl named Sue
She could never tell what was true
The town filled with hate
And sad was her fate
Now she knows not what to do

Legal Eagle

There once was a town called Eagle
Where everything done was all legal
But all of their files
Became shredded piles
When they were chewed up by a beagle

Cory the Horse

There was a young horse named Cory
Who wanted to be a star in a story
But his master John
Worked him all day long
So Cory never starred in a story

Poor Mac

There was an old man named Mac
Who had a big kink in his back
When the old man went lame
His mind did the same
And he died one day in his shack

Party

Party time USA
Having fun, night and day
You tell me of times to come
When there won't be room to run
You tell me, bro, the time is near
When man and beast will live in fear
What I want to say in this rhyme
Is that I believe it's party time
No more pushing for the power
No more building our tombstone tower
Living is just a space to fill
Whether it's good or bad is our will
Youth is the time for fun
Finding our fortune in the sun
Love thy neighbor, bro of mine
Don't take him for his last dime
Believe in the fun and good things
In this world full of human beings
So if the lives of all are wrong
Our faith in good isn't strong
So get together, have a blast
Make life good while it lasts
Well, I'll cut the tune to go torch
Out in back or on the porch

Let's all party
Night and day
Party, party, party
Take the blues away

(1976)

Reality!

I lay in a field among flowers of yellow
Lying and dreaming, peaceful and mellow
Life is a fairy tale when I'm in this state
Nothing worries me, my problems don't relate

Then down comes reality like a dense, dark cloud
I'm quickly overcome by the encircling shroud
I struggle, and I fight, and I cry out loud
Is it that I'm too humble, or am I too proud?

I can't comprehend the vicious circle I'm in
I've lost the beginning and I can't find the end
Sometimes it's almost like being buried alive
And I'm always wondering how I'll ever survive

Then I fully awaken from my brief nap
I pull myself together, give myself a slap
I finally realize with a thought that gave me chills...
It's just a fact of life, I'm going to have to pay my bills!!!
(1982)

The Search

Though weary as I've traveled far
My spirit leadeth me on course
To find the girl who evaded me
To finalize our divorce
(1977)

Travelin'

(Haiku)

This Long old Hi-way
I'm in a cruise control daze
Are we there yet, Dad?

Truckin' On Down the Line

(Sort of based on the tune of Lodi by CCR, first verse to chorus)

I really wish I had a dollar
From every place I've stayed
I'm like a rolling tumbleweed
Not worrying about the cards I've played
I really love what the world provides
To help me ease my mind
But I gotta' keep on truckin'
Truckin' on down the line

Now I just checked out of Cherokee
Trying to see what I could see
But all I found was a bunch of cheats
Trying to get all they could out of me
So I turned my tail and lost that town
Just as fast as I could go
And I'll never go back for a long, long time
That is one thing I know

I'm making my way to Alabama
Just to have myself some fun
To find me a chick and live it up
Then turn my back and run

I know it's bad to be that way
But it's just the way I live
I can't settle down and take a wife
Because my life is too much to give

Maybe someday I'll settle down
After seeing enough of the world
But for now I have got to go
And see what my future holds
Maybe someday the perfect girl
Will make me want to stay
But that time has not yet come
So I'll be on my way
(1975)

Nature

Clouds

I lie in a field for hours
The silence has wondrous powers
I love the sun a shining down
Not being near a noisy town

Then come the clouds one by one
And before long they cover the sun
I don't like the clouds all bunched together
And I soon hope there's a change in the weather

I work in the field all day
The sun is blazing away
I wish I was someplace cool
Instead of here like a fool

Then come the clouds to shade the sun
Oh, look now, I'll get my work done
The shade is great, there's no doubt
When the sun was burning, it tuckered me out
(1975)

Dark and Stormy

The day is dark, the wind is cold
Blowing the leafless trees
Swaying and bending, but standing bold
As a lone boat on the seas

The dark streets are cold and wet
Like ribbons round a painting
Against the dark sky this scene is set
As if for sale and waiting

The high line poles stand tall and straight
With their wires a weaving
Just like a drifter who cannot wait
And is just now leaving
(1975)

Gray and White

I sit in class, writing this poem
A looking out the window
The wind is blowing and it is snowing
A beautiful white snow

The trees are gray, the sky is gray
And only the snow is white
It sure looks gloomy with all that gray
But still, it's a beautiful sight

I sit in silence not making a sound
Except my pen a scratching
It isn't hard to understand things
When winter is a hatching
(1975)

Here Comes the Rain

The day is full
The sun is bright
Nothing is dull
In this wonderful light

But then comes the clouds
A floating in
The thunder is loud
And the rain soon will begin

Now it is raining
A heavy, heavy rain
The dog is straining
Against his chain

It had stopped by evening
But still all is wet
The clouds were leaving
As we watched the TV set

Tomorrow might be better
With the sun shining in
But it just might be wetter
If it does rain again

Now comes the night
The clouds are all gone
It sure was a sight
Though it didn't last long
(1975)

It's Springtime

The days are getting warmer
The time is getting right
Here comes the far-out springtime
We can rumble all day and night

You see the couples boogie
At the parties or at the show
Now you're sure it's springtime
The people let you know

When it comes to springtime
All the poets always say
You can tell by how the birds sing
But there is another way

You can tell by all the people
As the town gets to movin'
When they get down to the warm days
And really get to groovin'

So I don't know its springtime
When the squirrels come out to run
The squirrels can do their own thing
While I boogie down and have some fun
(1977)

Nature

The morning has broken over the hill
Bringing light to the hills and valleys
Lighting dark and lonely streets and alleys
The dew on the grass and the slight chill
This is a soft reminder of nature's will
When she above all of mankind rallies
With the power to light those hills and valleys
And bring the birds to your windowsill
But for sunshine alone she does not live
As we as her constant witnesses know
She also has her rain, her wind, and her snow
And all the storms she has the power to give
We all know too well that nature rules all
And she has the power to make mankind fall
(February 1976)

Quiet Strangler

He comes into the cities and towns
Spreading like a fog
He hangs in the air and all around
That ugly, filthy smog

He bellows out of pipe stacks
Spreading across the land
Against his force we cannot lack
To take the topmost hand

If he spreads too thick and far
He could kill us all
On our country he's the greatest mar
And he could make us fall

He comes into the cities and towns
Spreading like a fog
He hangs in the air and all around
That ugly, filthy smog
(1976)

Snow Feeling

The snow comes down
A sparkling white
It's all over town
With the coming of night

Oh, wondrous snow
You melt so fast
But your continuous flow
Makes you last and last

I love you so much
Even though you are cold
You'll always have this touch
Even as I grow old

So stay here with me
Through this lonely hour
Not too many people see
How your silence has power

Though the sun's heat
May make you melt
Your large white sheet
Is so deeply felt

I leave you now
To let you play
And I wonder how
You'll hear what I say
(1975)

Spring

Spring is here
So bright and clear
And the kids come out to play
The grass is green
The birds begin to sing
On this crisp and beautiful day
I love the spring
So bright and clean
It seems to show the way
"Just follow me
And you'll be free"
Is what spring seems to say
As time goes by
The bright blue sky
Tells us summer is on its way

(1975)

Springtime

Walking on a springtime day
It's enough to scare the blues away
Come on, friends, now whatcha say
Sure feels a lot like springtime

Here we go walking, you and I
On a bright clear day with a big blue sky
It makes me feel like I can fly
Sure feels a lot like springtime

I dig life as you all know
Not much more interest I could show
Can't you feel that cool breeze blow
Sure feels a lot like springtime

I'm gonna have fun galore this spring
Running around while the birds all sing
I don't know what summer will bring
But it sure feels a lot like springtime
(March 1976)

The Stream

The spring runs with the warming sun
With fleeting Shadows on the run

Through the mountains tall and free
Glittering like many suns upon the sea

The freedom that man attempts to tame
Its' beauty and glory his progress lames

Like so many other beautiful things
He seeks to destroy for the luxury it brings

But I continue to follow the fleeting streams
Like a lonely lady follows her fading dreams

I only hope that I'm not alive to see
Man make the last stream cease to be
(1977)

The Wind

The wind is blowing
The dust is in the air
Rising and then settling
As a drifter without a care

How I hate the wind
Blowing dirt in my eyes
Flopping things around
And messing up the skies

The sun hardly filters through
All the dust that's floating around
I sure wish the wind would stop
So the dust would finally settle down
(1975)

Inspirational

A New World

We call for freedom in his glory
For all his people under the sun
And for the past glory we have won
This be the making of a familiar story

No one in his eyes need to worry
For he above is the only one
That can help us finish what we've begun
And can bring us freedom in his glory

We pack our things, we plan to leave
It is only for his protection that we ask
For we and he know it be a difficult task
And it is in him and freedom we believe

So now we shall set out on our own
To a new world of freedom to make a home

(February 1976)

Always with You

You'll feel the warmth of his smile
In the sunrise each day
You'll hear his laughter
In the children as they play
Although he is gone physically
He's spiritually here to stay
You'll always be blessed with his presence
To help you in life, come what may

Rejoice in your time with him
Spent with you here on earth
Take comfort in the good things
And the memories since his birth
To know what's still to come
And to know what it is worth
When you come together again
In the Lord's immaculate church

Believe

Always try to live your life right
Be sure to keep your heart true
Believe in the good Lord above
And he will believe in you

Always hope for the best
Yet be prepared for the worst
Consider your own needs last
And always put your family first

Sometimes it's hard to keep faith
To believe he's just not there
Though life can still be a struggle
You must know that he cares

Believe in yourself
Believe in him
Believe in life
That begins again
(2014)*

---

* This poem was written for or inspired by inmates at a facility
where I work as a correctional officer.

Dreams

In the larger scheme of things
We all have to keep our dreams
Don't let 'em go—don't let 'em go-oh-oo

We must maintain humility
Live a life of tranquility
Go with the flow—go with the flow-oh-oo

I know sometimes it seems
We're just stuck in between
Can't let it show—can't let it show-oh-oo

Believe in a higher power
That evil will devour
Let people know—let people know-oh-oo

There are blessings from above
Showing us such true love
I'm sure it's so—I'm sure it's so-oh-oo

Keep your dreams true to heart
Never let the doubting start
Keep the faith stay true to Thee
And a home above will forever be!
(2015)

Friends Can Be

Friends can be
Two boys or girls
Or a mixture of the two
Friends can be
So many people
Or maybe just a few

Friends can be
Close or far
Or somewhere in between
Friends can be
Old folks or babies
Or people in their teens

Friends can be
Lovers or companions
Or partners in something
Friends can be
Someone who wants to see
How much happiness they bring

Friends can be
Two boys or girls
Or a mixture of the two
Friends can be
So many people
Or maybe just me and you
(1976)

I Love Life

I love life
To give and gain
I love life
Thru joy and pain

If you love life
I give you my hand
If you love life
You love the land

For people are life
I know for sure
And people can love
True and pure

War, is cheating
War, is lies
Wars are games
With power, the prize

I like a different power
That gives people ease
The power I like
Is the power of peace

Peace is something
We all can use
Peace is patience
So please don't refuse

I love life...
For you and for me
And I hope total peace
Is soon to be
(1975)

I'd Like to Write a Song

I'd like to write a song for you
That's free and flowing clear
I'd like to write it loud and long
For all the world to hear

My song will be of peace
Of love throughout the land
A song that makes you really think
To lead you by the hand

But all the songs I can write
And all the songs the world sings
Unless that lost and lonely bell
Of freedom is allowed to ring

So take your neighbors in your arms
And float and sway with the tune
Do not hesitate go right away
And the wars will end real soon

So I won't write a song for you
That's new and you haven't heard
I'll stick beside an older song
Of peace and freedom's word
(1976)

Mom on the Inside

For so long you've been stuck in here
So hard to believe it'll be over a year
Kept away from your friends and family
The toll on your heart is easy to see

Keep the faith and stay true inside
You've learned in his word to abide
Another life lesson he's challenged you
Stay strong until this test is through

Take your lumps with chin held high
It is far too late to question why
You know where it is you went wrong
And you know where it is you belong

To be there for your kids at home
To keep them safe and never alone
You must focus, live your life right
Keep the big picture in your sight

So here's my hope from me to you
Keep it in mind whatever you do
I want you to stay happy and free
And don't come here to visit me
(October 2015)*

---

* This poem was written for or inspired by inmates at a facility
where I work as a correctional officer.

Smile

When sometimes you're feeling down
And you think the world's against you
Just think of all the people around
What it'd be like if they were all blue

There'd be no booming laughter
Nor any giggles in between
There'd be silence from thereafter
And no smiles would ever be seen

So cheer up and be listening
To this tale of advice I tell
Just smile with your eyes a glistening
And then all will be quite well

Smile, when you're not happy
Smile, even when you are blue
Smile, and make it snappy
Smile, and I'll smile with you
(January 1976)

The Demon

(Haiku)

I know he is there
I fight with him all the time
The demon inside

I fight him so hard
But the victories are his
Formidable foe

He stands in my way
He keeps me from doing right
So I do nothing

He is so obscure
His power is so sublime
So intangible

My good intentions
Fall prey to hidden fury
He drives them away

Is it a sickness
Total lack of ambition
Maybe laziness

Is there a doctor
To help me eradicate
This demon inside

I believe there is
He is deep down in my heart
The good Lord above
(2010)

The Strongest Little Man

When days are bleak and hope is fading
May inspiration come from within
May your courage and fortitude
Allow complete healing to begin

Know that we are here with you
Our prayers, our thoughts, our desire
Know that you are not alone in this
That within us, the faith you inspire

For a soul so young and fragile
You possess the courage of a Saint
To endure what you've encountered
And fought on without complaint

May the good Lord soon reward you
May he pay it forward for all to see
May the blessings of your recovery
Bear witness to our belief in thee

Self

A Great Little Feeling

I've got a funny feeling
Something's gonna change
It's a great little feeling
Kind of alarming and strange

Somehow, sometime soon
I feel a dream coming true
That'll revoke all my depression
And end my feeling blue

I'm gonna make my way
And somehow do it right
Maybe this great little feeling
Will bring my guiding light

(1985)

A Poet

A poet says so many things
To make people understand
The happiness the world can bring
To everyone throughout the land

He writes of all the sorrows
And all the tears that fall
He writes of our tomorrows
And the future of us all

A poet is sincere
In everything he says
It may not be so clear
For he writes in many ways

So hail to the poet
For all the world to see
Even though I don't show it
A poet's what I want to be
(1976)

A Poet's Plea

I am a poet
I write what I feel
It isn't always right
It isn't always real

I say what I want
I don't hold it back
When it comes to spirit
There's not much I lack

I have my bad days
Like all the rest
More than some
Than others I've less

I try to write
So you'll understand
I want recognition
So give me a hand

I don't need enemies
I hate to hate
I'm just ordinary
And I'm sure not great

So if you don't like me
Or don't like what I write
I'm truly sorry
And please let's not fight

I want you to know
That I really do try
To treat people right
And be a nice guy
(1975)

Be My Friend

The whispering of the wind
The beat of a tune
Listening to my stereo
Staring at the moon

The wide open sky
The darkest of blue
Leads you to thinking
Of things you need to do

The sound of a late bird
Heard faintly through his song
Leads you to remember
The chances done gone

All the wasted time
Not spent on living fine
All the summer evenings
Seen through teardrops and wine

Be my friend now
Whoever is near
I don't have much left
To hold unto my own soul dear

A quiet lonely feeling
As quiet as the night
I don't get the feeling
I've lived my life right

The sound of more birds
Their tunes increasing in number
Proves a fast coming daybreak
And I with no slumber

The quiet summer evening
Through the night then come dawn
Takes me back to summer evenings
Done come and gone

My stereo's silence
Adds to the pain
Not a hurting pain
But of a life lived in vain

So be my friend now
On this night, solemn and free
But no one is near
Just the silence and me
(1977)

Confidence

In the realm of the invincible
In a world that could be a dream
To the eye it appears so majestic
To the soul it feels so serene

I've defeated all my weaknesses
I've surpassed unattainable goals
I'm respected by family and friends
I'm feared by those deemed my foes

As twilight engulfs my surroundings
The soft glow warming my domain
I could ask no more from my life
I will cherish all my years that remain

To be the envy of others
To be the apple of the eye
To be the Lord of my Kingdom
To be so free I could fly
(2014)

Contentment

Woke up this morning
With the sun shining in
I just couldn't wait
For the day to begin

Slipped on some clothes
And stepped into the light
It seemed like a day
Everything would go right

Got me some eats
To give me some pep
I felt better and better
Just great with each step

Spent all the day
Driving thru town
Just minding my business
Just bummin' around

Night came on fast
And ended the glare
Yet it still felt good
In the cool night air

Oh! Beautiful morning
Oh! Beautiful day
Oh! Beautiful evening
Chase the blues away!
(1975)

Crossroad

At a crossroad in my life
Decisions to be made
The support of my wife
I would never trade
It's now time for me
To decide what to do
I can no longer be
A slacker with a high IQ
Please pray for me.

—"D"
(2011)

Darkness

Darkness is falling
Casting shadows everywhere
All is gloomy
And without care

I hate the darkness
So lonely and blue
But it makes me happy
To see morning dew

The only way
The dark isn't bad
Is when I'm sleeping
But still all is sad
(1975)

Decisions

And in the sentences that I write
May I script exactly what I need to know
And in the comforts that I may afford
May also come the ability to grow
In these be our fleeting lifetimes
That succumb to the ticking clock
We must so quickly find the key
And quicker find the door to unlock
As I search what has been presented
Deciding if I take yet another chance
If I'm to look down another hallway
To another ballroom, another dance
Lord, I pray ye grant me the wisdom
To guide me and direct my future trail
At a time when the years are dwindling
To change course yet again should I fail
(2014)

Emotions

Don't know what I'm gonna do
All these emotions runnin' through
Demands and orders put on me
How am I going to make them see?

People tell me how good I am
When I don't even give a damn
They think I ought to be the best
But I'm just not like the rest

If they would only get off my back
I wouldn't be inclined to blow my stack
So please believe me when I say
I just can't go any other way

So stay away, don't jump my sh——t
Just be cool, and that will be it
If they just knew how it is with me
But I just can't make them see
(1977)

Forsaken

Forsaken by the world's cast
Beaten not for first, but last
Competing for stakes too low
Stuck in ruts no place to go

But an escape you can find
It lies within your own mind
Find the key and free the bond
To see the future, you must look beyond

(1977)

I Am Free

Whenever I get to feelin' down
And I find it's hard to get around
I think of this little rhyme

Birds fly high
They are free
Stop to rest
In a tree

I am free
I can't fly
But I can dream
And touch the sky

Fish swim deep
They are free
Swim to the deepest
Part of the sea

I am free
I can't swim deep
But I can breathe
And I can weep

Bears are big
They are free
Sleep all winter
In summer flee

I am free
I'm not big
But I can sleep
And that I dig

I am free
Inside and out
So what do I have
To gripe about
(1977)

I Got Friends

Lone and Ugly
In an ugly place
But I got friends
In any case

I got no chicks
No girls like me
They all back down
From what they see

Some guys like me
Others they don't
Some will trust me
Most others won't

I have a few friends
They seem to know
How much I care
Which way I go

I only want
To get along
And find a place
Where I belong

Lone and Ugly
In an ugly place
But I got friends
In any case
(1976)

I Try

I try to be a good man
I try to do what's right
I try in every way I can
I try both day and night

I like to stay back and find
What is the best thing to do
Storing all I see in my mind
So I know how to make it through

I try to play it really cool
To stay out of people's way
But I won't be no one's fool
That's one thing I can say

I do not like to fight
I don't want to make a scene
I feel that silence has great might
If you get what I mean

I try to be a good man
I try to do what's right
I try in every way I can
I try both day and night
(1976)

I'm Me

The wind whips my hair
As I sit here and think
So many things I'm not sure of
So many missing links

I realize my life is going
Much faster than it seems
I don't see how I can fulfill
All my lifetime dreams

I feel so much as I sit
I see so much in my mind
What is really my final goal?
What is it I hope to find?

I have my worries and doubts
But I have no qualms of fear
I just don't know about my life
Or even why I'm here

But I'll go forward on through life
And live and breathe and be
I don't know just where I'll go
I just know I'm me
(March 1976)

Incarceration

Made some choices, without a clue
I've done wrong, I know it's true
Done some things I shouldn't do
Now I'm here to pay what's due

When I'm free to walk the street
I've got to walk a different beat
I've got to make my life complete
Live my life righteous and discreet

Lessons I've learned the hard way
Should be lessons learned to stay
Learned and lived from day to day
It can't be just some game I play

These four walls contain me
But my faith will sustain me
My spirit will entertain me
No matter how much it pains me

This is my consideration
More than just a fascination
Do nothing without justification
And always avoid incarceration
(2014)*

---

* This poem was written for or inspired by inmates at a facility where I work as a correctional officer.

Independence

I tell my folks, I tell my friends
My life is mine to live
But they try to change my ways
And try to make me give

I bend a little here and there
To keep them satisfied
But they don't think I bend enough
No matter how I've tried

Now I will not try anymore
To be a perfect guy
I'll live my way, not bend at all
I'll not even try

And if my plan doesn't work at all
I'll have to try again
A whole new plan in all respects
Is what I will begin

This new plan is really quite simple
I'll just do all they request
But I'm sure my plan right now
Is sure to be the best

I now will end this little rhyme
And begin my perfect plan
Without heeding a word they say
I'll bug them all I can
(1975)

Looking Inward

As I go through my life
I've slowly come to realize
It's what's in the heart
Not what's in the eyes
It's not about what you see
It's about what you feel
Not about how pretty
Only about what's real
It's not about what you got
But about what you give
Not about your power
But about how you live
We usually know what's right
But is that what we do
Do we get ahead with a lie
Or really gain by being true
You've got to look inside
And see what's really there
You got to know yourself
Find out if you really care

I'm learning every day
To change my philosophy
To sincerely think of others
Not just be concerned with me
(2015)

My Contribution

I am trying to decipher an intangible code
Working to help set free a struggling soul
Am I that insightful, knowledgeable, and bold?
Can I alone influence them with my control?

They come into my presence full of arrogance
Believing they know so much more than the rest
Yet they are so very lost in their own ignorance
Not knowing in reality they are failing the test

Thinking they're an indestructible and formidable being
That they have the lead in this, their life's dance
The answers are there, but they are not seeing
Letting escape what may be their last chance

Can I be an influence on their future decisions?
Can I even one iota of a difference make?
Can I steer their course with an invisible precision?
Can I instill in them the importance of what's at stake?

I make the effort to not just a keeper be
To provide a symbol, or an example yet
Distant goals, a light for in darkness see
A beacon of determination, lest they forget
(2014)*

---

* This poem was written for or inspired by inmates at a facility
where I work as a correctional officer.

My Soul

As I sit looking deep into my soul
I wonder about decisions I have made
If this is the place I should really be
The chances presented begin to fade

I seem to grow older with increasing speed
The years seem to be just flying by
Drive and determination they elude me
I'm left sitting here wondering why

I'm a real role model for procrastination
Thinking so hard, but accomplishing naught
So now in the twilight of my lifetime
My life's decisions have left me distraught

I feel I have so much more potential
And I've left myself short in life's exchange
Is it too late to reverse my fortune?
Have a chance to correct and rearrange

I must rededicate my future efforts
I've got to make some hard choices
I've got to change my life's direction
Until my deep inner soul rejoices
(2014)

Myself

Some people would say
They can't understand my way
And I hope they never do
Because then I would be through

Some people just know
How their life will go
But my life is my own
To wherever I may roam

I dig the way I live
Because it's easy to give
All my love and hate
Without any form of wait

So if you ever feel
My life isn't real
I hope you will see
To me, I'm just me, and that's enough for me
(1976)

One Time

Once I was a young man
I did what I saw best
To please me for the moment
No consideration for the rest

Now all of those good times
Those times without a care
Are gone without a trace
As if they were never there

Only the memory of chances
That I let slip right on by
I was young and carefree
Didn't think I'd have to try

Now I have to struggle
Just to break an even pace
Once so far out in front
Only in the end to lose the race

My one-time friends have faded
Like my one-time blue jeans did
And I think back and I wish
That I was still that carefree kid

One time I had the world on a string
The earth was lying at my feet
But I got that string wrapped round my neck
Now I'm old, and tired, and beat
(March 1976)

Poor Boy

I'd like to take a trip
I'd like to go away
To Canada or Mexico
Or other places far away

I'd like to be a rich man
I'd like to own a castle
But I'm just a poor boy
And just to live is quite a hassle

I'd like to be a movie star
I'd like to play the screen
With rhinestones on my cowboy hat
Leather suits that look real mean

I'd like to be most everything
The best in every way
But I can only continue life
And hope for success someday

'Cuz I'm just a poor boy
Who has a lot of dreams
Maybe someday they'll come true
But they won't the way it seems
(1976)

Self-Pity

I'm here at the end of my Rainbow
And there is no pot of Gold
There is no great redemption
There is no great sight to Behold

Just me and the sum of my life's decisions
Stretched out before my mind's eye
A collage of small triumphs and big regrets
A little bit of truth and a whole lot of lie

They say the road paved of good intentions
Is but a wide and winding highway to hell
The good I had always wished to accomplish
Couldn't be achieved by casting a simple spell

So here I sit alone with my disappointments
My potential now buried deep in the past
My "Time to Shine" is a time gone by
I should have known that time doesn't last

All that is left is to ask for divine forgiveness
To ask for his Mercy upon my sad soul
To hope he highlights my few good points
And ignores when the evil had control

So the colors of the rainbow are fading
The sun no longer a prism of the mist
The darkness is enveloping my lifetime
Waiting for death, my lips to be kissed
(2014)

Shining Moonlight

Shining moonlight
Falling star

Sit and wonder
Who you are

Times were good
Times were bad

Sit and think about
What you've had

Sit quiet and secure
At peace at ease

Nowhere to go
No one to please

Can't it be like this
Day after day?

Will there ever be
A better way?

(1987)

Super Star

Super Star
Sing a song
Whoever you are
You won't last long

Playing cool
Quiet, with a style
Shining fool
Recognized awhile

Super guy
Ten feet tall
Can touch the sky
Long hard fall

Standing back
Playing it smart
On the right track
But missed the start

Don't play cool
Quiet with style
You're just a fool
Recognized awhile
(1976)

The Midnight Ship

I'm riding on the midnight ship
The only one to take the trip
Summer air, the skies so clear
Nothing against me, nothing to fear

The ship, she sails slow and free
Without passengers or crew, just me
She sets her course and travels far
Trying to catch some distant star

In perfect rhythm she rocks to and fro
I'm not sure how far she'll go
But then it lightens with a gleam
And I awaken from my dream
(1976)

Time in a Bottle

Time in a bottle
Floating by

On the sea of life
I wonder why

Always knowing
Receive and send

Someday knowing
It's come to an end

Time in a bottle
Each in breath

Just existing
Until death!
(1988)

Time

Time goes by
I'm flying high
I am rising, to the sky

Now and then
Descent would begin
But soon I would rise again

I look down
At the cities and towns
And all the people running around

Life's so fast
It just doesn't last
Soon the future will be the past

I need some time
To make a dime
But time, just isn't mine

The sinking sun
The day is done
I am glad I had some fun

So now the end
Is just round the bend
And my scars I cannot mend

Time goes by
I'm flying high
I am rising, to the sky

And death, I know, is nigh
(1975)

Time to Change

In a cold and solitary world
Freedom just but a thought
A "count down the days" existence
Regret the wrong and getting caught

All the time inside your head
The swirl of what went down
Wishes of things done different
Some way to turn it all around

Looking for options to change
Of a future of different outcome
As a leopard changing his spots
A truly better person to become

Time may be of the essence
But they say it is never too late
A chance to prove the old adage true
Good things come to those who wait
(October 2015)*

---

*   This poem was written for or inspired by inmates at a facility
where I work as a correctional officer.

Yourself

Before you can believe in others
Give of your love and your heart
You must learn to believe in yourself
This is where your journey must start

You can fly all around the world
You can travel both near and far
Just always remember this one thing
Wherever you go, there you are

If you just can't live with that one person
Whom you will have to face all of your days
The one person you can't run away from
Then you might need to change your ways

You can be your own worst enemy
Or you can become your best friend
Because no matter where you go
You're stuck with yourself in the end
(2015)